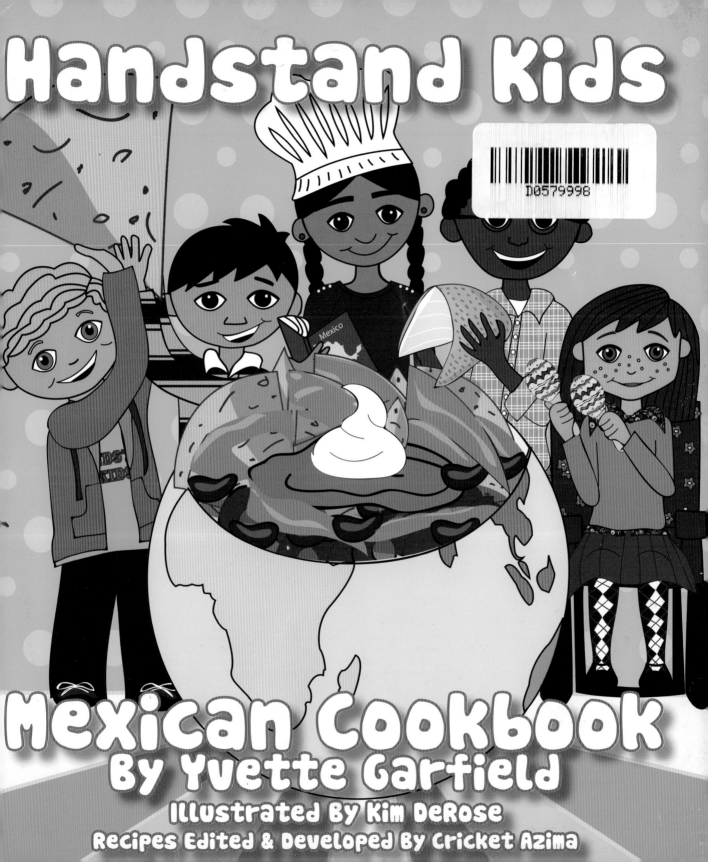

Handstand Kids

Mexican Cookbook
By Yvette Garfield
Illustrated By Kim DeRose
Recipes Edited & Developed By Cricket Azima

Published by Handstand Kids, LLC

Printed In China.

ISBN: 978-0-9792107-2-3

By Yvette Garfield

Illustrated By Kim DeRose

Designed By Vani Sodhi Gundara

Recipes Edited & Developed By Cricket Azima

Editing By Avital Binshtock

U.S.A.

Tijuana

Gulf of California

Cuidad Juarez

Guaymas/
San Carlos

Chihuahua

México

Loreto

Monterrey

Gulf of Mexico

La Paz

Cabo San Lucas

Mazatlan

Isla
Mujueres

Mérida

Cancun

Puerto Vallarta

Guadalajara

Playa del Carmen

Cozumel

México City

Manzanillo

Cuernavaca

Veracruz

Ixtapa/
Zihuatanejo

Pacific Ocean

Acapulco

Oaxaca

Belize

Huatulco

Guatemala

Honduras

El Salvador

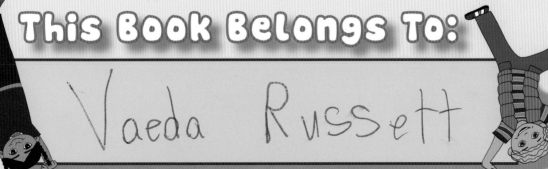

This Book Belongs To:

Vaeda Russett

Dedication

This book is dedicated to my parents whose infinite amount of love and humor inspire me to do what I do.

Special Thanks

To everyone who worked on this book, thank you for taking this amazing journey to Mexico with me.

THANK YOU!

3

Table of Contents

A Child's Introduction To Food Happens in The Home
A foreword by Chef Aarón Sanchez

A child's introduction to food happens in the home, and creating food-related memories can be pivotal in bringing families closer together.

When I was a young boy growing up in a Mexican family, food always played a central role for us. The time put into preparing meals together allowed me to form an intense bond with my family. While I can't always remember the specific dishes we cooked, I can vividly remember how happy and nurtured I felt during those times in the kitchen; it was a haven for being with my family and friends, and it kept me grounded.

Children look to their families during their formative years in order to become healthy, happy, productive people. The *Handstand Kids Mexican Cookbook* will continue a legacy of cooking with the family and preserve a rite of passage that every child should experience. Especially in today's fast-paced world of convenience and sensory overload, cooking and eating still represent an arena in which we can teach our children to appreciate taking the time to prepare a healthy and delicious meal that passes traditions from one generation to the next.

I only wish I had had a cookbook like this to reinforce my growing love for preparing food for others. I am confident that the *Handstand Kids Cookbooks* will not only open new doors for kids, but also provide a foundation that will enrich them for the rest of their lives.

Chef Aarón Sanchez,
Co-host of Food Network's *Melting Pot*, New York restaurateur, author of the cookbook *La Comida del Barrio*, and one of *People* magazine's most beautiful people

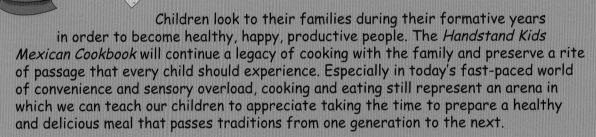

Utensils
in English and Spanish:

Blender

Liquadora

Bowls (large, medium and small)

Cuenco (grande, mediana y pequeña)

Can Opener

Abrelatas

Cutting Board

Tabla de Cortar

Fork

Tenedor

Knife

Cuchillo

Grater

Rallador

Serving Plate

Plato de Servir

Measuring Cup

Taza de Medir

Measuring Spoon

Cuchara Dosificadora

Saucepan (large and small)

Sarten (grande y pequeño)

Soup Pot

Olla

Spatula

Espátula

Spoon

Cuchara

Tongs

Pinzas

Whisk

Batidor

Wooden Spoon

Cuchara de Madera

Ingredients in English and Spanish:

Apple
Manzana

Avocado
Aguacate

Beans
Frijoles

Bread
Pan

Butter
Mantequilla

Carrots
Zanahorias

Cheese
Queso

Chicken
Pollo

Cinnamon
Canela

Eggs
Huevos

Garlic
Ajo

Lettuce
Lechuga

Lime
Lima

Milk
Leche

Oil
Aceite

Onion
Cebolla

Rice
Arroz

Salt and Pepper
Sal y Pimienta

7

Sour Cream	Sugar	Tofu	Tomatoes	Tortillas

Crema Cortada	Azúcar	Tofu	Tomates	Tortillas

Recipe Levels: Avocados

Look for the avocados at the top of each recipe to determine the recipe's level of difficulty. Each recipe is ranked between levels 1 and 4; more avocados means that more adult help is encouraged.

Remember, an adult supervisor must be in the kitchen at all times!

 1 avocado means that this is a basic recipe and that you can do most of the steps yourself.

 2 avocados means that the recipe is a little bit harder and there are some steps that an adult will need to help you with.

 3 avocados means that an adult will need to handle certain steps.

 4 avocados means that an adult will need to help you with the entire recipe.

8

Stir It Up!

Congratulations on becoming a Mexican chef!

Not only is it fun to make these foods, but it is wonderful to use your new cooking skills to make others feel better. Try making some of these recipes for your friends and family.

Your cooking skills can also be used to help those in need. Local charities and food banks may accept food donations and youth volunteers; check the Handstand Kids website for volunteer opportunities: www.handstandkids.com.

Remember that your new cooking skills can help change the world!

Introduction

Welcome to the Handstand Kids cookbook series! Food is a fun and hands-on way to learn about people around the world and other cultures. By learning Mexico's recipes, you are opening your kitchen to a world of experiences. While people around the world have many differences, they all have delicious foods and recipes that are special to their region.

The Handstand Kids (Ari, Felix, Gabby, Izzy and Marvin) will introduce you to Mexican cooking. While making some of Mexico's tastiest and most nutritious recipes, you will be introduced to Spanish, which is the language of Mexico. You will be on your way to becoming a Mexican chef!

After each recipe in this book, there is an alternative suggestion that encourages you to add your own favorite flavors and creativity.

An adult supervisor must be present in the kitchen at all times to assist kid chefs, especially when cooking over the stove or using sharp objects. Adult supervision will ensure that kid chefs are always safe.

Cooking is a fun, wonderful skill that you can use to help people. Making a special meal for a loved one will make their day! Bake sales and food fundraisers are also wonderful ways to raise money for a local group. In this book, the Handstand Kids characters hold a food fundraiser, selling tacos to raise money for Common Threads, an organization that educates disadvantaged children about the value of healthy eating while fostering an appreciation of cultural diversity through cooking. Many charities allow youth volunteers to help those in need. Check the Handstand Kids website for volunteer opportunities: www.handstandkids.com.

It is my hope that the Handstand Kids cookbook series will provide you with a fun and tasty way to learn about other places and people, and that the Handstand Kids inspire you to help make the world a better place.

So join the Handstand Kids as they travel the world, one recipe at a time!

Adios!
Yvette Garfield

Meet The

IZZY

Birthday February 8

Hey! I'm Izzy and I'm ten and a half years old. I like spaghetti a lot, But everyone says I am the pickiest eater that they know. I think I will also like enchiladas. It will be so fun to make them.

It will be so cool to make apple taquitos for my sister! She is a diabetic so she doesn't eat food with sugar. I want to make her this dessert because it's made without any sugar. I think she will love them!

FELIX

Birthday July 5

Greetings! I'm Felix and I am nine years old. I am starting a new school next year and they offer cooking classes after school. I am a vegetarian which means that I don't eat any meat. My whole family is vegetarian so we all love having lasagna for holidays. It will be awesome to make the Mexican version of lasagna called chilaquiles.

I have never cooked anything before and I really want to learn how to make guacamole and salsa. I can eat it for an after-school snack and make it for my friends.

Handstand Kids

GABBY

Birthday October 7

Hi! I'm Gabby and I am eleven years old. My favorite thing to do is learn new languages. So far I can speak three languages pretty well; English, Spanish, and Farsi. I absolutely love learning new words and I hope that one day I can speak to everyone in the world in their native language. I know that's ambitious, but I am starting young.

I am super excited to learn more Spanish words. I have been to Mexico twice and it would be great to visit again. My new favorite food is fiesta corn and I can't wait to make it at home while speaking Spanish!

MARVIN

Birthday April 19

Hi! I'm Marvin and I want to be a chef when I grow up. I'm only ten so I have tons to learn. My mom teaches me a lot of stuff when she's cooking. She has traveled a lot so we make all different kinds of food. When I was eight, she took me to Italy and I loved eating the panini sandwiches. I can't wait to make Mexican sandwiches called tortas. My mom says I will like them just as much as panini sandwiches.

One day I will have my own restaurant and serve all kinds of sandwiches.

ARI

Birthday December 17

Hello there. My name is Ari and I am eight years old. I love to eat all kinds of foods! My family thinks I am funny because I will try almost any food.

Last Thanksgiving, my family volunteered at a homeless shelter and we gave meals to a lot of families. I know the shelter takes food donations and I am really excited to learn new recipes to bring to them. I am also excited to hold food fundraisers for Common Threads! I think it's great that they teach kids about nutrition and how to cook. My favorite food of all time is cookies and I can't wait to make and share Mexican wedding cookies. Yum!

12

13

All Kids Love ....

Farmer's Market Chips, Pico de Gallo Salsa and Guacamole

15

Level 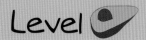   Serves 6

Ingredients   # Instructions

4 plum tomatoes **(tomates)**
2 ripe Hass avocados **(aguacates)**,
halved and pitted
2 limes **(limas)**, halved
½ white onion **(cebolla)**
1 cup fresh cilantro leaves
Salt and pepper
1 teaspoon jalapeno (optional)

Instructions for Pico De Gallo Salsa
1. Wearing the plastic gloves, dice the
tomates, cebolla and optional jalapeno.
Place them all into the medium bowl.

2. Chop the cilantro leaves and add to
bowl.

3. Cut one **lima** in half, squeeze the juice
into the bowl and mix well.

4. Add salt and pepper to taste.

**At this stage, you've made pico de
gallo! Continue on to make it into
guacamole...**

5. Spoon the **aguacate** meat into a bowl
and use a fork to mash it into your
desired texture.

6. Cut one **lima** in half, squeeze the juice
into the bowl and mix well. Then add the
pico de gallo to the **aguacate** and mix.

7. Add salt and pepper to taste.

Tools

Cutting board
Fork
Knife
Measuring cups
Measuring spoons
Medium bowl
Plastic gloves
Wooden spoon

Alternative

For mango salsa, dice 1 mango and add to Step 1 for a
fruity version of the **pico de gallo**.

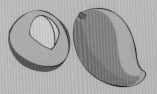

 Felix Says: "My family goes to the farmer's market once a week
to buy all our fruits and vegetables. It's so cool to try a new
veggie every week. I tasted cilantro for the first time this year
and I love it!"

x

Ingredients

12 6-inch corn tortillas
1½ pounds tilapia fish fillet
3 plum tomatoes **(tomates)**
½ small red onion **(cebolla)**
2 limes **(limas)**
1 cup fresh cilantro leaves
1 tablespoon cumin
¼ cup olive oil **(aceite)**
Salsa
Salt and pepper

Tools

Cutting board
Knife
Measuring cups
Measuring spoons
1 medium bowl
2 skillets
4 small bowls
Spatula

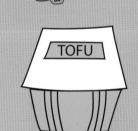

TOFU

Alternative

Substitute the fish with another protein food like beef, chicken or tofu.

Instructions

1. In the medium bowl, coat the fish with **aceite** and cumin. Add salt and pepper to taste.

2. Squeeze 1 **lima** over the fish.

3. Chop the red **cebolla** and the cilantro. Dice the **tomates**. Place the **cebolla**, cilantro and **tomates** in separate small bowls and set aside.

4. Cut the other **lima** into wedges. Place the wedges into a small bowl and set aside.

5. Place one of the skillets over a medium-high heat, and cook the fish in it for about 5 minutes on each side, or until the fish is cooked through and flakes with a fork. Remove the skillet from heat and set aside.

6. Heat the tortillas by placing them in the other skillet over a medium-high heat for 5 minutes or until warm.

7. Assemble each taco by filling a tortilla with approximately 1/3 cup of fish and a teaspoon each of cilantro, **tomate** and **cebolla**. Squeeze a **lima** wedge over each taco. Add salsa to taste.

 Ari Says: " I love using my new cooking skills to volunteer. I bet we can sell enough tacos to help a lot of kids!"

Ranchero Salsa
Ingredients

8 plum tomatoes (**tomates**)
1 medium onion (**cebolla**), peeled and quartered
3 garlic (**ajo**) cloves, peeled
Salt and pepper
Chips (optional)

Tools

Blender
Cutting board
Knife
Large skillet
Wooden spoon

Instructions

1. Slice the **tomates**, **cebolla** and **ajo**, then set aside.

2. Heat the large skillet over a medium-high heat. Place the **tomates**, **cebolla** and **ajo** into the skillet and cook for 10 minutes, or until the **tomates** appear clear. Stir with the wooden spoon.

3. Pour the vegetables and their juices into the blender and purée until smooth.

4. Pour the purée into the skillet and bring to a boil. Reduce to a simmer and cook for 5 minutes.

5. Add salt and pepper to taste.

6. Cool and serve with the chips, or continue on to use the ranchero sauce for the enchiladas (see recipe above).

Enchiladas
Ingredients

12 6-inch corn tortillas
1 large yellow onion (**cebolla**)
2½ cups shredded Monterey Jack or Mexican cheese (**queso**) blend
2 cups cottage cheese
3 to 4 cups ranchero sauce (see recipe, left)
2 tablespoons olive oil (**aceite**)
½ cup sour cream

Tools

Aluminum foil
Casserole dish
Cutting board
Knife
Measuring cups
Measuring spoons
Medium bowl
Small skillet
Wooden spoon

Instructions

1. Preheat oven to 350 degrees.

2. Dice the **cebolla** and set aside.

3. In a small skillet, heat the **aceite** over medium heat. Then sauté the **cebolla** in the **aceite** for 6 minutes, or until the **cebolla** appears clear. Remove the skillet from the heat, then carefully pour the **cebolla** into the medium bowl and set aside.

4. Add 2½ cups **queso** and 2 cups cottage cheese into the medium bowl of **cebollas**. Mix together with the wooden spoon. This will be the **queso** filling.

5. Coat the bottom of the casserole dish with a thin layer (about ¾ cup) of ranchero sauce.

6. One by one, lay the tortillas flat on a cutting board. Spoon ⅓ cup of the **queso** filling evenly in a line down the center of each tortilla.

7. Take the right edge of the tortilla and fold ⅓ of the tortilla over the center.

8. Take the left edge of the tortilla and fold ⅓ over the center, making an envelope.

9. With the seam facing downward, place each folded enchilada into the casserole dish.

10. Cover the enchiladas with the rest of the ranchero sauce and sprinkle them with the remaining ½ cup of **queso**.

11. Cover with aluminum foil and bake in the oven for 15 to 20 minutes, or until the **queso** is melted.

12. Serve each enchilada with a dollop of sour cream on top.

Izzy Says:
" These enchiladas are so good! I eat them for dinner and then take the leftovers to school for lunch."

Alternative

Make this dish healthier by using reduced-fat **queso** and plain yogurt instead of sour cream.

Chicken With Rice Never Tasted So Nice
(Arroz con pollo)

Ingredients

1 pound chicken (**pollo**) breast (about 3 to 4 breasts)
2 cups rice (**arroz**)
1 garlic clove (**ajo**)
4 cups chicken broth
1 large onion (**cebolla**)
1 can diced tomatoes (**tomates**), with juice
1 green pepper
1 tablespoon cumin
1 bay leaf
¼ cup vegetable oil (**aceite**)
1 teaspoon salt
½ teaspoon pepper

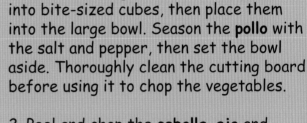

Tools

Cutting board
Knife
Large bowl
Large pot with lid
Measuring cups
Measuring spoons
Oven mitt
Wooden spoon

Instructions

1. On the cutting board, cut the **pollo** into bite-sized cubes, then place them into the large bowl. Season the **pollo** with the salt and pepper, then set the bowl aside. Thoroughly clean the cutting board before using it to chop the vegetables.

2. Peel and chop the **cebolla**, **ajo** and green pepper and set them aside.

3. In a large pot, heat the **aceite** over a medium-high heat. Add the **cebolla**, **ajo** and **arroz**. Wearing the oven mitt, stir continuously for 2 minutes.

4. Add the **pollo**, broth, **tomates**, green peppers, cumin and bay leaf. Stir to combine.

5. Bring to a boil for 5 minutes. Then reduce heat to low and cover with lid. Cook for about 35 minutes, or until **pollo** is cooked, **arroz** is soft and broth is absorbed.

Alternative

Substitute the **pollo** with a vegetarian option like tofu. Try brown rice for a healthier version.

 Gabby Says: " This recipe helps me learn how to say 'chicken with rice.' Now I ask my mom to help me make *arroz con pollo* for dinner."

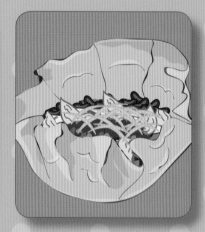

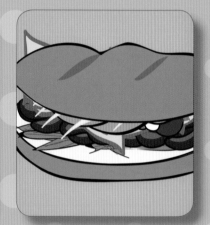

Nutritious

&

Delicious

Tasty Enough to Eat the Bowl... Shredded Chicken Tostada

Level

Serves 6

Ingredients

1 pound cooked, shredded chicken (**pollo**)

6 prepared tostada shells

1 15-ounce can of refried beans (**frijoles**)

½ head romaine lettuce (**lechuga**), shredded

2 plum tomatoes (**tomates**)

½ cup grated Monterey Jack cheese (**queso**)

1 lime (**lima**)

1 cup cilantro leaves

½ cup red wine vinegar

¾ cup olive oil (**aceite**)

Sour cream

Guacamole

Salsa

Salt and pepper

Tools

Can opener
Cutting board
Fork
Knife
Measuring cups
Small bowl
Whisk

Instructions

1. Shred the **lechuga** and set aside.

2. Dice the **tomates** and set aside.

3. Assemble the tostadas by layering the ingredients in the following order: tostada shell, small scoop of **frijoles**, approximately ½ cup shredded **pollo**, a handful of **lechuga**, ¼ cup diced **tomate**, a sprinkle of cilantro, and a sprinkle of **queso**.

4. In the small bowl, combine vinegar, **aceite**, **lima**, salt and pepper, to taste. Whisk together to create the dressing.

5. Pour the dressing over each tostada.

6. Garnish with sour cream, guacamole and salsa to taste.

Alternative

Make a vegetarian version by skipping the **pollo** and simply adding more **frijoles**!

 Gabby Says: "This salad is so much fun to eat because you get to eat the tostada bowl and there aren't any dishes to bring to the sink when I am done eating."

 26

Level  Serves 4 – 6

Ingredients

4 8- or 10-inch flour or corn tortillas

1 15-ounce can refried pinto beans **(frijoles)**

1 cup shredded Monterey Jack cheese **(queso)**

Salsa

Tools

Can opener
Large skillet
Measuring cups
Small skillet
Spatula
Wooden spoon

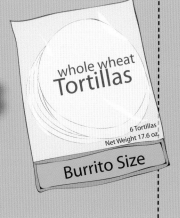

Instructions

1. Pour the **frijoles** into the small skillet. Heat over a low-medium heat, stirring occasionally.

2. In the large skillet over medium heat, warm the tortillas until softened, then remove them from the skillet.

3. Using the spatula, spread $\frac{1}{4}$ of the **frijoles** onto each tortilla.

4. Sprinkle $\frac{1}{4}$ cup **queso** over each tortilla.

5. Fold the bottom of the tortilla upwards and each side inwards to form the burrito shape.

6. Add salsa to taste.

7. Serve while hot.

Alternative

For a low-cholesterol option, try shredded soy **queso** instead of Monterey Jack.

Marvin Says: "Burritos started in the Mexican state of Chihuahua. The word "burrito" means "little donkey.""

There's Meatballs (Albondigas) in My Soup!

Albondigas ROCKS!

29

Level    Serves 4 – 6

Ingredients

6 cups chicken stock
1 pound ground beef
5 carrots (**zanahorias**)
1 28-ounce can diced tomatoes
(**tomates**) with juice
1 medium yellow onion (**cebolla**)
1 egg (**huevo**), beaten
1 lime (**lima**)
1 garlic (**ajo**) clove
1½ teaspoon cumin
1 bay leaf
1 teaspoon salt
½ teaspoon pepper

Organic Free Range Chicken Broth

Tools

Cutting board
Knife
Ladle
Large soup pot with lid
Measuring cups
Measuring spoons
Medium bowl
Nonstick baking sheet
Spatula
Wooden spoon

Instructions

1. Preheat oven to 375 degrees.

2. Dice the **cebolla** and set aside.

3. Mince the **ajo** and set aside.

4. In the medium bowl, combine the ground beef, **ajo**, **cebolla**, cumin, salt, pepper and **huevo**. Cut the **limas** in half and squeeze their juice into the bowl. Mix well with spatula, then form into 1- to 1½-inch balls (about 15 meatballs).

5. On the nonstick baking sheet, cook the meatballs in the oven for about 10 minutes, or until browned. Remove from oven and set aside.

6. While the meatballs are cooking, cut the **zanahorias** into thin slices.

7. In the large soup pot, heat the **tomates** (with their juice), **zanahorias**, chicken stock and bay leaf over a medium-high heat and bring to a boil.

8. When the meatballs are out of the oven, transfer them from the baking sheet into the large soup pot.

9. Reduce the heat and allow the soup to simmer for 20 minutes before serving.

Alternative

Make a low-fat version by using ground turkey or **pollo** instead of beef. Or, for a vegetarian soup, try making soy meatballs and using vegetable broth.

 Felix Says: "I love to make this soup for my family with soy meatballs! We buy soy meatballs at the grocery store and follow the easy instructions on the package. Most of my friends can't even tell that they aren't made of meat."

Fiesta Corn

It's *fiesta* time!

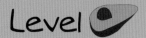
Ingredients

2 cups canned corn kernels
1 small yellow onion **(cebolla)**
1 green pepper
1 red pepper
1 cup button mushrooms
1 lime **(lima)**, halved
½ cup fresh cilantro leaves
1 tablespoon olive oil **(aceite)**
Salt and pepper

Tools

Cutting board
Knife
Large skillet
Measuring cups
Measuring spoons
Wooden spoon

Alternative

Spice up this dish by adding a diced chili pepper into the skillet with the corn! When dicing the chili pepper, wear plastic gloves and make sure to wash your hands well when done dicing.

Instructions

1. Dice the **cebolla** and peppers and set aside.

2. Slice the mushrooms and set aside.

3. Chop the cilantro and set aside.

4. In the large skillet, heat the **aceite** over medium heat.

5. Add the **cebolla** and cook for 5 minutes, or until the **cebolla** looks clear.

6. Add the peppers and mushrooms, stirring them in with the wooden spoon. Cook for 4 minutes.

7. Add the corn and cook for another 3 minutes, or until all vegetables are soft.

8. Add salt and pepper to taste.

9. Squeeze the **lima** over the vegetables.

10. Stir in the cilantro and serve.

 Ari Says: "Fiesta corn is my favorite Mexican dish because it's like a veggie party on your plate."

32

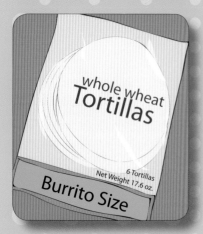

whole wheat
Tortillas

6 Tortillas
Net Weight 17.6 oz.
Burrito Size

Mexican-ize My....

Chips into Nachos

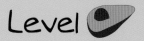

Ingredients

1 large bag corn tortilla chips

1 15-ounce can refried pinto or black beans **(frijoles)**

2½ cups shredded cheddar, Monterey Jack or Mexican blend cheese **(queso)**

2 tomatoes **(tomates)**

1 cup salsa

1 cup guacamole

½ cup sour cream

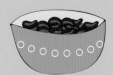

Tools

Can opener

Cutting board

Casserole dish

Knife

Measuring cups

Small skillet

Instructions

1. Preheat oven to 350 degrees.

2. Dice the **tomates** and set aside.

3. Pour the **frijoles** into a small skillet and heat over low heat until warm.

4. Place the chips in the casserole dish.

5. Pour the **frijoles**, **queso** and **tomates** over the chips and place the casserole dish in the oven. Bake until the **queso** melts (about 12 to 15 minutes).

6. After removing the casserole dish from oven, top the nachos with salsa, guacamole and sour cream.

Izzy Says: "Nachos are the best to eat at a soccer game. In Mexico they call soccer fútbol, so nachos are also my favorite food to eat at fútbol games."

Alternative

For a low-fat version, use reduced-fat **queso**, or cut the amount of **queso** in half and add 1 diced bell pepper.

Level    Serves 4

Ingredients

4 8- or 10-inch flour tortillas

2 cups shredded Monterey Jack or Mexican blend cheese (**queso**)

½ cup salsa

½ cup guacamole (optional)

¼ cup sour cream (optional)

Tools

Knife

Large nonstick skillet

Measuring cups

Spatula

whole wheat **Tortillas**

6 Tortillas
Net Weight 17.6 oz.

Burrito Size

Instructions

1. Place the tortillas flat and sprinkle ½ cup **queso** on half of each.

2. Fold the tortillas in half to cover the **queso**.

3. Place the tortillas in the large skillet and cook over a medium-high heat until one side is lightly browned (about 2 to 3 minutes).

4. Use the spatula to flip the tortillas and cook the other side until lightly browned and the **queso** has melted. Remove from heat.

5. Cut into triangles and serve with salsa, guacamole and sour cream.

Alternative

Add cooked veggies into the tortillas when sprinkling in the **queso**. Try bell peppers, mushrooms and **cebollas** for new flavor combinations.

 Felix Says: "Quesadillas are so fun to make for parties. My whole family eats them with all kinds of veggies because we are vegetarian. Once, my brother put 12 different kinds of vegetables in his quesadilla and we all clapped for him."

Level

Ingredients

4 sourdough or French bread **(pan)** rolls, halved

1 pound beef, cubed or shredded

1 15-ounce can refried pinto beans **(frijoles)**

1 cup iceberg or romaine lettuce **(lechuga)**

1 avocado **(aguacate)**, halved and pitted

½ cup salsa

¼ cup shredded Monterey Jack cheese **(queso)**

Tools

Can opener
Cutting board
Knife
Measuring cups
Medium skillet
Wooden spoon

Instructions

1. Place beef in the medium skillet, cover with a layer of water and bring to boil over high heat. Reduce heat to medium and simmer until meat is thoroughly cooked. Drain, cool and set aside.

2. Shred **lechuga** and thinly slice aguacate and set both aside.

3. Slice the **pan** rolls in half horizontally. On the bottom half of each **pan** roll, spread the **frijoles**, then layer the beef, **lechuga**, aguacate, salsa and **queso**.

4. Place the top half of each roll on the fillings and serve.

Marvin Says: "When my friends ask me what kind of sandwich I brought for lunch, I tell them it's a torta!"

Alternative

For a vegetarian **torta**, skip the beef and add more **aguacate**, **frijoles** and **queso**.

Level    Serves 4

Ingredients

4 cups corn tortilla chips
6 eggs **(huevos)**
1 cup shredded Monterey Jack
cheese **(queso)**
1 small white onion **(cebolla)**
1½ cup salsa (green or red)
2 tablespoons vegetable oil **(aceite)**
Sour cream
Salt and pepper

Tools

Cutting board
Knife
Large skillet
Measuring cups
Measuring spoons
Small bowl
Whisk
Wooden spoon

Alternative

Stir in a handful of cooked,
shredded chicken to the
huevos while they are
cooking in the skillet.

Instructions

1. Dice the **cebolla** and set aside.

2. Crack the **huevos** into the small bowl
and whisk.

3. In a large skillet, heat the **aceite**
over a medium-high heat. Add the diced
cebolla to the skillet and cook for 3
minutes, or until it appears clear.

4. Add the **huevos** and salsa, stirring
while cooking to scramble them.

5. When the **huevos** are almost cooked
(about 5 minutes), stir in the tortilla
chips and the **queso**.

6. After the **huevos** are cooked, add salt
and pepper to taste.

7. Serve with sour cream and salsa or hot
sauce on top.

Gabby says: "My grandmother makes
the most amazing chilaquiles for Cinco
de Mayo. That means 'Fifth of May,'
which is the date on which we celebrate
Mexican culture with food, music and
dancing!"

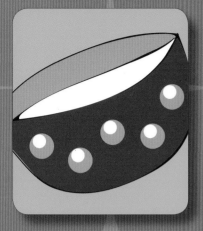

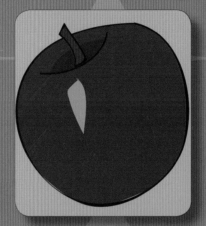

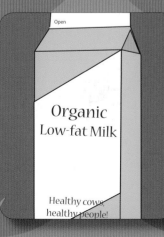

Save Room For ...

Ingredients

6 8- or 10-inch whole-wheat tortillas

1 large apple (**manzana**)

1 cup applesauce

¼ cup vegetable oil (**aceite**)

1 teaspoon cinnamon (**canela**)

Tools

Cutting board

Knife

Measuring cups

Measuring spoons

Medium bowl

Nonstick baking sheet

Pastry brush

Instructions

1. Preheat oven to 350 degrees.

2. Dice the **manzana** on the cutting board. Mix the diced apple with the applesauce and **canela** in the medium bowl using the wooden spoon.

3. Use the pastry brush to lightly coat both sides of the tortillas with **aceite**.

4. Place 1 heaping tablespoon of the **manzana** mixture in the center of each tortilla.

5. Roll the tortillas to make a flute shape, then place them on the baking sheet.

6. Bake for 20 minutes or until the tortillas become crispy. Then remove them from the heat and let cool.

7. Sprinkle a little **canela** on top of each warm taquito.

Alternative

Add ½ cup raisins to the **manzana** mixture or serve with a scoop of vanilla ice cream!

 Felix Says: "I love desserts with fruit in them. My mom says I am supposed to eat 5 pieces of fruit a day and dessert is a fun way to eat them!"

46

Ingredients

2 cups flour
1 cup butter **(mantequilla)**, softened
1 cup confectioners' sugar **(azúcar)**
1 cup ground nuts (almonds or pecans)
1 tablespoon water
2 teaspoons vanilla extract
¼ teaspoon salt

Tools

Measuring cups
Measuring spoons
Medium bowl
Nonstick baking sheet
Small bowl
Spatula
Spoon

Alternative

In a microwave-safe bowl, melt 8 ounces of chocolate chips in microwave. Drizzle the chocolate over the cookies and let the chocolate harden before serving.

Instructions

1. Preheat oven to 325 degrees.

2. In a medium bowl, mix the **mantequilla**, vanilla extract and ½ cup of the confectioners' **azúcar**.

3. Stir in the flour, salt and nuts. Stir in the water to help the dough come together. Mix well until the dough is formed.

4. Use your hands to roll the dough into 1-inch balls. Place the balls on the baking sheet.

5. Bake for 15 minutes, until the cookies are set but not browning. Remove the baking sheet from the oven. Then use the spatula to remove the cookies from the baking sheet. Allow them to cool slightly.

6. Pour the remaining ½ cup of confectioners' **azúcar** into the small bowl. Roll the cookies through the **azúcar** so that they get coated with it. Serve.

 Gabby Says: "When I went to my cousin's wedding in Mexico last summer, I ate so many of these cookies that my cousin joked that I would be the next girl in the family to get married."

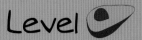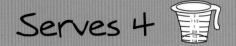
Ingredients

1 cup dark or semi-sweet chocolate

4 cups low-fat milk **(leche)**

1 teaspoon vanilla extract

½ teaspoon cinnamon **(canela)**

Tools

Ladle

Measuring cups

Measuring spoons

Medium saucepan

Microwave-safe bowl

4 mugs

Whisk

Instructions

1. Break up the chocolate into small pieces and place into the microwave-safe bowl.

2. In the microwave, heat the chocolate for 1 minute or until melted.

3. Meanwhile, heat the **leche** in the medium saucepan over a medium-low heat.

4. Once the **leche** is warm, add the melted chocolate and whisk together until consistency is smooth.

5. Add the **canela** and vanilla and stir. Add more **canela** or vanilla as desired.

6. Ladle into the mugs and drink.

Alternative

Sugar-Free

Chocolate

100g.

Try using sugar-free chocolate.

 Marvin Says: "Mexican hot chocolate is my favorite drink to make in the wintertime. I make it for my friends when they come over for the holidays. Everyone cheers for me when I serve it because they love it so much!"

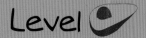
Ingredients

8 8- or 10-inch whole-wheat tortillas
½ cup sugar (**azúcar**)
½ cup vegetable oil (**aceite**)
2 tablespoons cinnamon (**canela**)

Tools

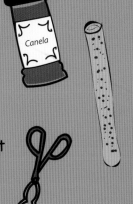

Cutting board
Knife
Measuring cups
Measuring spoons
Nonstick baking sheet
Small bowl
Small spoon
Spatula
Tongs

Alternative

Instead of using **azúcar**, try dipping the baked strips in honey.

Instructions

1. Preheat oven to 350 degrees.

2. Cut the tortillas into strips.

3. In a small bowl, combine the **canela** and **azúcar** with the small spoon and set aside.

4. Place tortilla strips onto the baking sheet. Drizzle them with **aceite**.

5. Sprinkle the strips with the **canela-azúcar** mixture, making sure to coat both sides of each strip.

6. Bake for 5 minutes. Then, with the tongs, flip the strips over. Bake for another 5 minutes. Remove the baking sheet from the oven when the strips turn a light golden brown.

7. Immediately sprinkle with additional **canela** and **azúcar** mixture if desired and serve.

Izzy Says: "My sister loves dipping her *buñuelo* sticks in honey. Your hands get sticky but it's so worth it."